P9-DHN-236

[Eclectic School Series]

# THE ECLECTIC PRIMER;

FOR

# YOUNG CHILDREN.

DESIGNED TO PRECEDE

Wm. H. McGUFFEY'S

## ECLECTIC READERS.

- 1836 -

CINCINNATI:
PUBLISHED BY TRUMAN AND SMITH,
150 Main Street.

## ROMAN NUMERALS EXPLAINED.

A numeral is a symbol meaning number. Our system of counting is believed to have begun by people counting on their fingers. Both the Arabic (1, 2, 3, 4, etc.) and the Roman (I, II, III, IV, etc.) are believed to have started this way. The word digit, meaning number, is from the Latin word digitus, meaning finger. The number V (5) seems to be representative of an open hand; and, the number X (10) seems to be like two open hands.

In earlier days, our forefathers used the Roman system to indicate chapter headings in books. To help you understand those numbers more easily you may refer to the chart below:

| Roman | Arabic | Roman | Arabic | Roman | Arabic |
|---|---|---|---|---|---|
| I | 1 | XI | 11 | XXX | 30 |
| II | 2 | XII | 12 | XL | 40 |
| III | 3 | XIII | 13 | L | 50 |
| IV | 4 | XIV | 14 | LX | 60 |
| V | 5 | XV | 15 | LXX | 70 |
| VI | 6 | XVI | 16 | LXXX | 80 |
| VII | 7 | XVII | 17 | XC | 90 |
| VIII | 8 | XVIII | 18 | C | 100 |
| IX | 9 | XIX | 19 | D | 500 |
| X | 10 | XX | 20 | M | 1000 |



Mrs. Jean Morton, Editor



For information about other Mott Media publications visit our website at www.mottmedia.com.

ISBN-13: 978-0-88062-018-5
ISBN-10: 0-88062-018-8

## PRESENT PUBLISHER'S PREFACE.

Out-of-print for over 125 years, the *original* McGuffey's Eclectic Readers are considered educational classics. These books are world renowned for their teaching of reading through the integration of faith with learning.

William Holmes McGuffey, outstanding 19th century educator and preacher, combined both of his God-given talents in the preparation of these early textbooks. Millions of copies were sold in their *original* Christ-centered form. The character of our Nation was molded in an upright manner through the repeated use of these textbooks over several generations.

In order to capture the true spirit of the *original* McGuffey's Eclectic Readers we have made no major content changes. While this edition of the *authentic* Readers is being presented in a more easily readable form, the stories, poems, and pictures appear as they did in the first edition.

Slight changes have taken place for the sake of clarification. However, no changes have been made in editorial content.

The Publisher wishes to express his heartfelt appreciation to the staff of the Special Collections Library at Miami University, Oxford, Ohio, for its cooperation in researching the *authenticity* of this book. Additionally, we desire to thank Dr. John H. Westerhoff, III, for his inspiration in promoting the republishing of the *original* works and Bohn Printing for their untiring efforts in typesetting the Readers.

It is indeed an honor and distinct pleasure to return the *original* McGuffey's Eclectic Readers to you. The content of this series will help you develop outstanding reading skills, Christ-centered character, a love of good literature, and impressive speaking abilities. I am sure you will find the *original* McGuffey's Eclectic Readers to be a valuable teaching tool whether they are used in the public school, Christian school, or for those who choose to teach their children at home.

George M. Mott, Founder
Mott Media

## ROMAN CAPITAL LETTERS.

A B C D

E F G H

I J K L

M N O P

Q R S T

U V W X

Y Z &

## ROMAN SMALL LETTERS.

| | | | |
|---|---|---|---|
| a | b | c | d |
| e | f | g | h |
| i | j | k | l |
| m | n | o | p |
| q | r | s | t |
| u | v | w | x |
| | y | z | |

## ITALIC CAPITAL LETTERS.

*A B C D*

*E F G H*

*I J K L*

*M N O P*

*Q R S T*

*U V W X*

*Y Z &*

## ITALIC SMALL LETTERS.

*a* *b* *c* *d*

*e* *f* *g* *h*

*i* *j* *k* *l*

*m* *n* *o* *p*

*q* *r* *s* *t*

*u* *v* *w* *x*

*y* *z*

# LESSON I.

BOY

# MAN

# HEN

# TOP

# LESSON II.

HAT

# RAT

# CAT

# POT

# LESSON III.

| | |
|---|---|
| BOY | POT |
| boy | pot |
| MAN | HAT |
| man | hat |

HEN RAT

hen rat

TOP CAT

top cat

## LESSON IV.

It is he.

We do so.

He is up.

So is he.

You do so.

Go to her.

We go in.

Oh, it is.

It is so.
So am I.
If we do.
I am on.
On we go.
Lo, it is.
I am he.
Is it so?

---

| | | | |
|---|---|---|---|
| it | he | is | we |
| so | up | in | if |
| go | to | am | oh |
| on | you | her | do |

# LESSON V.

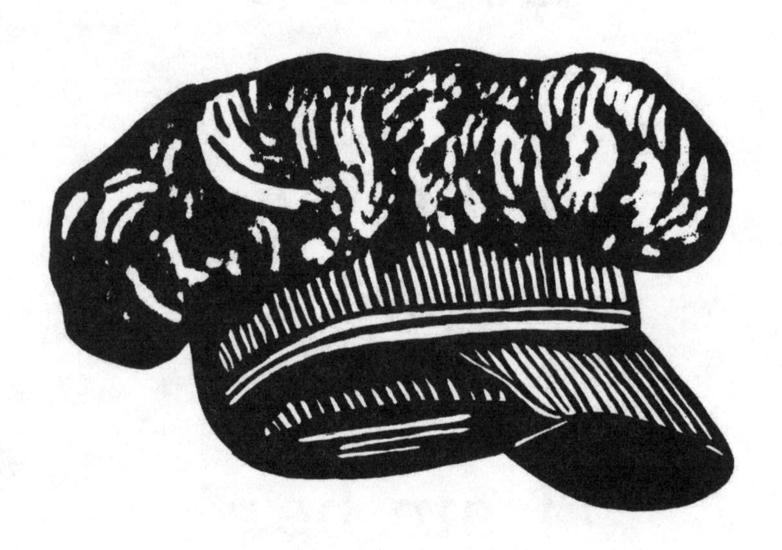

CAP

cap

# FOX

# fox

JUG

jug

# APE

## ape

# COW

cow

# HOG

# hog

# LESSON VI.

He ran up to us.

I did not see him.

How old are you?

Try to do the sum.

The hen can fly.

It can not fly far.

The sun is now up.

The sky is red.

You may all go out.

Do not go far.

---

| | | | |
|---|---|---|---|
| out | her | see | may |
| him | off | age | dry |
| why | put | ten | sky |
| you | run | sum | day |

## LESSON VII.

His pen is new.

It has a bad tip.

I can cut it off.

Dry up the ink.

Why do you cry so?

The hat was new.

Her cap is put up.

We can run to her.

We saw him go by.

He was in his cart.

---

| | | | |
|---|---|---|---|
| his | cut | cap | see |
| pen | ink | her | are |
| new | him | off | age |
| can | saw | spy | tip |

# LESSON VIII.

A FAN is
for girls.

A GIRL
can walk.

A KITE is for boys.

A TRAP is for mice.

A GOAT has long hair.

A BIRD will fly in the air.

| | | |
|---|---|---|
| girl | walk | kite |
| trap | mice | will |
| bird | goat | gives |
| loud | sound | bell |
| boys | why | hair |
| | has | |

# LESSON IX.

Let us go out.

Do not run, it is so hot.

The dog has bit the pig.

Oh, dog, do not do so!

You must put the pig in the sty.

Do not let the dog get to him.

He has bit his ear. See, it is red.

Now we may go to see the sick man.

He is so ill he can not get out of bed.

Old man, can you eat a bit of my roll?

If you can, I will give it to you.

---

| | | | |
|---|---|---|---|
| do | run | sty | get |
| he | hot | ear | one |
| us | you | pig | him |
| oh | get | see | give |
| my | dog | old | will |
| the | air | put | sick |
| who | ill | bed | roll |
| now | man | | |

# LESSON X.

*Boy and Dog.*

Do you see the dog?

I see the boy and the dog.

The dog has long ears.

The dog barks at the boy.

He will not bite him.

Do not pull the dog's tail.

If you do, he will bite you.

The dog has four legs, and two ears.

---

| | | | |
|---|---|---|---|
| do | you | boy | and |
| if | see | dog | has |
| he | and | him | barks |
| at | two | pull | bite |
| but | ears | will | four |

# LESSON XI.

My son, do no bad act.

Go not in the way of bad boys.

A bad boy has woe. He can have no joy.

If you tell a lie, you will be a bad boy.

If you do ill, few will care for you.

If you do well, all will love you.

To have the love of all will give you joy.

If you can not love, you must not hate.

Do not try to hurt him who is a foe,

For God can do to him as He will.

Let it be your joy to do the will of God,

For He can see you, and all you do.

son
for
few
way
lie
all
love
boy
you
hurt

God
you
bad
not
act
him
give
your
who

can
joy
hate
boys
have
tell
must
and
may

# LESSON XII.

*Boys and Girls at Play.*

Here are six little boys and girls.

See them go round, round, round.

Yes, but you must not go round too fast.

You may fall down and get hurt.

Boys and girls must not be rude in play.

Ah, now they must stop.

The school bell calls them away.

---

| | | | |
|---|---|---|---|
| are | boys | girls | little |
| six | and | them | round |
| bell | may | fast | must |
| get | fall | girl | away |
| but | rude | now | school |

## LESSON XIII.

*The Sick Little Girl.*

Do you see that little girl?

Yes, I see her. She is sick in bed.

Her mother is by her side.

She can not help her.

Can you help the little girl?

No! No one can help her but God.

You may get sick, and I may get sick.

We must ask God to help us when we are sick.

---

| we | and | but | God |
|---|---|---|---|
| yes | see | her | that |
| she | sick | side | mother |
| can | help | may | soon |
| not | bed | all | little |

# LESSON XIV.

*The Tea Party.*

Ah, little girl what have you here?

We have a little tea party.

Will you take a cup of tea?

No, I thank you, pass it to Ann.

Ann and Jane will each take a cup.

Hold the spoon in your right hand.

Do not let your cup fall.

How kind and happy these little girls all seem to be.

---

| | | | |
|---|---|---|---|
| ah | will | what | little |
| all | pass | girls | thank |
| not | kind | fall | spoon |
| let | hand | right | these |
| cup | each | seem | happy |

# LESSON XV.

## *Boys at the Pump.*

Here are boys at the pump.

How many boys are there?

I see one, two, three boys.

One boy has hold of the pump.

John has a cup in his hand.

I use a small cup when at tea.

One of the boys has no cap.

What has he done with his cap?

Ah, there it is at his feet.

What are caps made of?

Some caps are made of cloth, and some are made of skins.

Of what use are caps?

They keep our heads warm, that we may not take cold.

Is your head warm? Do not let the cold wind blow on it.

Do not take off your cap when out of doors.

You may catch a cold and get very sick.

---

| | | | |
|---|---|---|---|
| here | small | what | jump |
| boys | feet | done | many |
| head | have | warm | there |
| caps | your | cloth | three |
| take | doors | skins | pump |
| wind | blow | keep | John |
| sick | feet | they | keep |

# LESSON XVI.

*Cows in the Field.*

What do you see here?

I see one, two, three cows.

The cow does not work.

She gives us sweet milk.

A cow is not so large as an ox.

The cow eats grass and hay and corn.

She has four legs and four feet.

The cow does a great deal of good.

The cow is kind and will not hurt you.

Are you fond of milk? Oh yes, I like milk. It will make us grow.

You must not hurt the cow.

Oh, no, I will not hurt her.

Good boys will not hurt the cow.

We must not hurt any beast. God made the cows, and God made us.

Bad boys hurt the cow. God does not like the ways of bad boys.

---

| | | | |
|---|---|---|---|
| cow | four | two | three |
| kind | large | corn | great |
| work | gives | milk | sweet |
| hurt | make | grow | must |
| will | does | made | any |
| like | boys | fond | bad |
| you | field | what | large |
| the | eats | and | good |

## LESSON XVII.

*The Man and his Horse.*

Here is a fine horse.

See how he pricks up his ears!

The man holds him fast.

Now he will have a ride.

The man has a whip in his hand.

You must not go too near the horse.

The horse will kick with his feet.

He can walk, or trot, or run.

You must be kind to the horse.

A horse will plow in the field.

Let us go into the field, and play.

We will play upon the grass.

How sweet the grass is in spring!

The horse is fond of grass.

So is the cow and the ox.

The grass is made into hay.

A colt is a young horse. Some colts are quite small.

A horse can draw a cart or a coach.

Do not go near the cart, as it may run over you.

---

| | | | |
|---|---|---|---|
| here | fine | horse | how |
| pricks | ears | man | hold |
| fast | have | ride | whip |
| hand | near | walk | draw |
| coach | must | field | sweet |
| young | quite | spring | fond |
| come | plow | play | small |
| and | you | kind | now |

# LESSON XVIII.

## *The Setting Sun.*

Look at the sun! See, it sinks in the West. Who made the sun?

It was God, my child. He made the sun, the moon, and the stars.

God made each tree and herb, the tall oak, and the low bush.

God bids the trees to put forth their leaves, and at His word they fade and fall.

He bids the wind to blow, and He bids it to cease.

I can not see the wind, yet it blows round me on all sides.

So God is with me at all times, and yet I see Him not.

God sees and knows all things. He sees me when I rise from my bed. He sees me when I go out to work or play, and when I lie down to sleep.

If God sees me, and knows all that I do, He must hear what I say.

Oh, let me speak no bad words, nor do any bad act; for then God does not like bad words or bad acts.

---

| | | | |
|---|---|---|---|
| sun | look | words | sinks |
| who | made | noon | each |
| fade | work | trees | forth |
| him | wind | times | blow |
| hear | must | when | knows |
| cease | things | round | leaves |

* Original 1836 Advertisement